CORGI ACRES

Written by
Tracy Thompson

Illustrated by
Stacy Jordon

Vabella Publishing
P.O. Box 1052
Carrollton, Georgia 30112
www.vabella.com

©Copyright 2024 Tracy Thompson

All rights reserved. No part of the book may be reproduced or utilized in any form or by any means without permission in writing from the author. All requests should be addressed to the publisher.

Manufactured in the United States of America

ISBN 979-8-89450-019-5

To purchase books:
Amazon
teacakebooksllc@gmail.com

Teacake Books LLC

Dedicated to
all of the staff who gave, and continue to
give, compassionate and professional care to
our corgis. Y'all are the greatest!
Bremen Animal Hospital
Carroll County Animal Hospital
Northwest Ga. Veterinary Emergency Ctr.
UGA Animal Hospital

Love to
my husband Mark, who is totally responsible
for locating each corgi baby. I love them all!

Thanks to
Beverly Bruemmer for making my dreams
come true. You are a great coach!
To Stacy Jordon for bringing all my
ideas to life. Denise Stewart for being
our tireless groomer.

Hi, my name is **Mallard Denardo Thompson.**
I am a Pembroke Welsh Corgi.
I was born May 29, 2019, in Leeds, Alabama.
I came to live in Georgia when I was eight weeks old.

My people are NCIS fans,
which is why I have this
super long name.
If you have a hard name,
I feel your pain.

My first home was a box with my fur mama.

My second home was a camper with my people. It was a tiny home, before there were tiny homes.

I would be bathed in the tub and then zoom from one end of the camper to the other trying to get the water off. A bath can make you feel really good. I would attack my toys and bark with excitement.

In order for me to live inside, I had to learn to potty outside and NOT on my people's rugs.

For a little guy, this is hard work, but I loved my treats, so I followed the rules.

I had doctor appointments and shots just like my people. This was not always fun, but again I loved my treats.

Once, I had to have surgery and that was my first sleepover away from my people. I missed them terribly. I was so glad I got to go home the next day. Yeah!

Growing up can be scary and fun. On my first birthday, I got a super scary present . . .

...a baby sister!
I did not like her at first.

Her name was **Lacy Victoria Thompson** and she was born in Kentucky, August 12, 2020. She was three months old when she came to live with us. She smelled like horses and talked funny.

I was jealous of all the love my people showed Lacy. It took a few days for me to appreciate my new playmate.

It turns out, girls are great at tug of war and ball chasing. I also got to be a big brother and teach her the rules.

The potty rule was very important because I wanted her to live inside with me. She was a fast learner.

Later, when we went to the doctor, I wasn't the only one who got shots. I explained to her about the treats. Sure enough, she got some too.

Lacy also had surgery and experienced her first sleepover. I missed her. It was so sad sleeping alone.

We went to get her later that week and it was great to have her back home.

I was the BIG brother and it was my job to prepare her for BIG things. I told Lacy it was time to celebrate her first birthday and that she would get a baby sister just like I did.

Boy, was she mad when all she got was a bag full of toys. What was up with that? People are sure hard to figure out!

Lacy was mad at me for days about the SISTER thing, but she soon forgave me.

It was not fun playing alone. Being forgiven was great. I got to play with all the new toys too! We played chase until we collapsed into a tired heap and then napped.

Naps are great because they rest your body and give you more energy to play.

If you are wondering why my people loved corgis, it is simple. They fell in love with Queen Elizabeth's corgis. They loved to watch the Queen walk her fur babies. They were so cute with their short legs and pointy ears.

I explained this to Lacy and she thought it was wonderful to be so special. Me too!

Lacy was now one year old and I was two. We were allowed to go for rides on the side-by-side. The rides were great. The wind would blow our ears backward and our tongues would hang out.

It was super fun to be speeding down the highway instead of walking on a leash. I was older, so I had to be cool. Lacy would dance, drool, and bark until she was hoarse.

The only evenings we didn't ride was when water was dripping from the sky. We were told that it was too messy and wet. This confused us because those were our two favorite things.

Four months later, a sad thing happened. I got really sick and had to go to the hospital and doctors almost every week. I had two more surgeries and my body hurt a lot. I didn't feel like playing and Lacy didn't understand why her big brother was sleeping or resting all the time.

The doctor told my people that I had a pancreatic disease. For the next nine months, we were hopeful that I would get better, but two months before my third birthday, I got my wings and crossed over the rainbow bridge.

At first, I was terribly confused. I could see my people and Lacy, but they couldn't see me. Then, I came to understand that I was an angel. I could not be on the Earth again, but I could watch from Heaven. Everyone was so sad and Lacy was alone. She had no one to play with.

Two days passed and on Wednesday morning, I saw my people load Lacy into the truck and travel to Draketown, Georgia. I was wondering what was so special that Lacy got to go, when I saw a barn come into view. It was huge with many stalls for animals.

When they walked into the barn, I heard whining and little whimpers. **WOW**, those guys look just like me! My people took one of those little boys and put him in the truck with Lacy.

It was then that I understood that Lacy now had a new baby brother to play with. On the way home, he was given the name
Gibbs McGee Thompson.
Gibbs had been born in Georgia, January 16, 2022, and was now six weeks old.

Lacy was no longer a little sister. She was now a BIG sister and would have to do the same job with Gibbs that I had done with her.

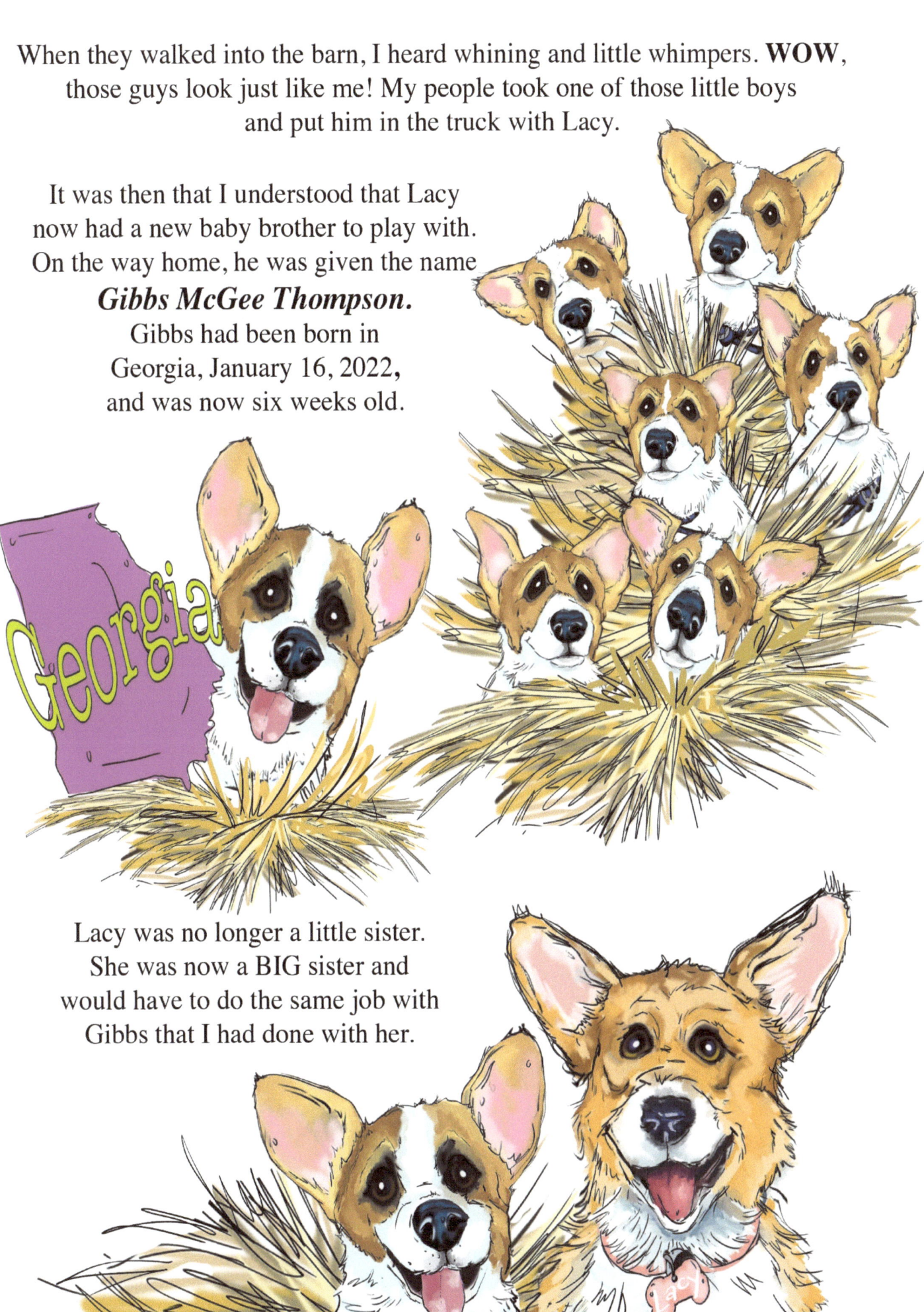

This is not the end of our journey, but it is Lacy's job to tell you the rest of the story. I will be flying around and enjoying my new and improved body. I might even eat a teacake or two with all of my new friends.

For four weeks, I helped my people train him to walk with his leash and potty outside. He is very calm for a puppy and has a very serious face with big brown eyes.

His nickname is Sad Eyes.

Gibbs has to go to the doctor and get shots and medicine too. It seems that this is normal for all corgis. I worry when he is away. I am very vocal! My sadness or happiness is easy to hear.

Gibbs just looks at me and wonders what all the fuss is about. I think we compliment each other, like the icing on a teacake.

Gibbs brought happiness and laughter back into our home. It was my job to protect and play with him. He would run from me and hide under the sofa so I couldn't reach him. He was super funny!

Six months later, it was my people's wedding anniversary. You'll never guess what they adopted! YEP, two baby boy Pembroke Welsh Corgis. They were born March 7, 2022, in Guntersville, Alabama. They came to live with us in Georgia, July 28, 2022, when they were four months old. They also got NCIS names.

One was called
Torres Tobias Thompson and the other **Vance Palmer Thompson**.

They were not red and white like us.
They were tri-colored, black, tan, and white.

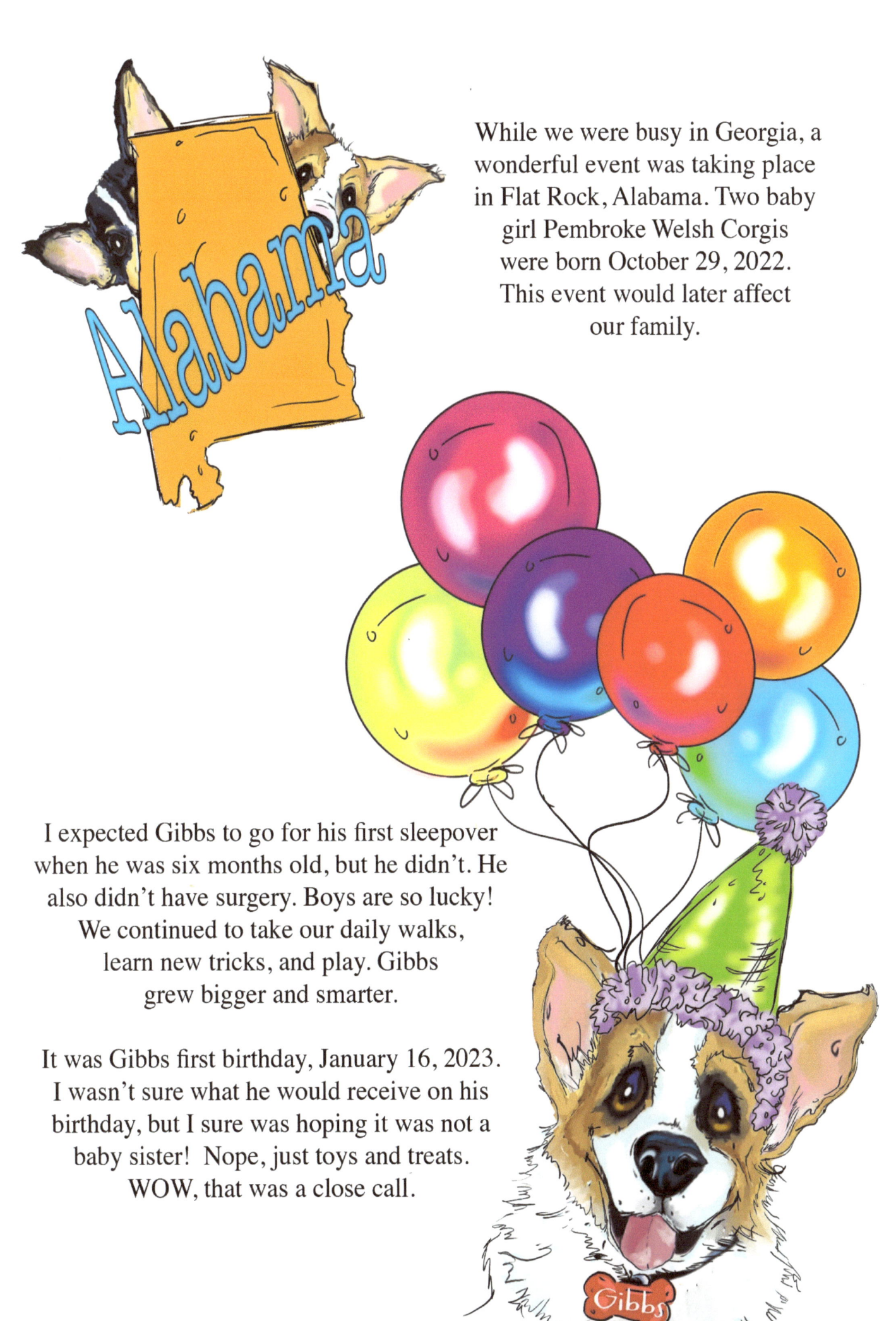

While we were busy in Georgia, a wonderful event was taking place in Flat Rock, Alabama. Two baby girl Pembroke Welsh Corgis were born October 29, 2022. This event would later affect our family.

I expected Gibbs to go for his first sleepover when he was six months old, but he didn't. He also didn't have surgery. Boys are so lucky! We continued to take our daily walks, learn new tricks, and play. Gibbs grew bigger and smarter.

It was Gibbs first birthday, January 16, 2023. I wasn't sure what he would receive on his birthday, but I sure was hoping it was not a baby sister! Nope, just toys and treats. WOW, that was a close call.

It was chaotic around here for a while until we got those boys settled. My people had to buy more leashes, walking jackets, bowls, food, and toys. A fence had to be erected and a kennel built because these boys were not staying in the house.

We had to teach them to come in and out of the kennel, to potty, and play. They were loads of fun and now I had three baby brothers.

Vance and Torres also had to go to the doctor and get shots and medicine. They didn't have surgeries or sleepovers when they were six months old either!

Well, I think I have figured it out. Boys have been exempted from sleepovers because they get homesick.

What do you think?

Vance and Torres grew bigger and smarter too. They made everyone laugh with their playful personalities.

We celebrated Vance's and Torres' first birthdays March 7, 2023. They got toys and new collars, but no baby sister. Hmmm? Maybe I was going to be the only girl in this family. It did have its perks and I got to be the boss since I was older. We settled in and developed a routine and everyone was happy.

Little did I know how my world was about to change.

Have you ever heard the phrase "the more the merrier?" Well, remember those two Alabama girls? YEP, on May 28, 2023, they came to live with us in Georgia. They were seven months old.

Since the NCIS saga had to continue, they were named
Ellie Kate Thompson and Abbie Grace Thompson.

You won't believe what happened the second day they were here! YEP, off for a sleepover. I was right all along. We girls are the only ones who can go away and not get homesick.

Talk about over drive, those girls were in hyper drive. Chaos took on a whole new meaning at Corgi Acres. Nothing was safe anymore. If it was chewable, it was chewed. If it could be caught, it was chewed. If it made a noise, LOOK OUT!

I was annoyed with these girls. They took our quiet and comfortable world and turned it upside down.

The girls stayed in the kennel and pen with Vance and Torres. They got along very well with the boys and settled into their own routine. Me and Gibbs were still living inside. Gibbs loved to go out and play with them for hours, but I did not like being chased and barked at by those five little siblings. I preferred my soft chair and quiet house.

Now there were six of us to take to the doctor, give medicines to, and take to the groomer. ***We loved medicine time because it was wrapped in cheese. YUMMY!*** All of us corgis were super smart, but my people learned fast too. They never took more than two of us out at a time and the groomer was scheduled to come to Corgi Acres. We didn't leave home unless the doctor had to give us shots or we needed tests to ensure our hearts were healthy.

The best time of any day was when my people came outside and opened the gate. We all ran and jumped into their laps and gave them kisses and hugs until we were pooped. We would lay on the cement porch floor and pant from the exercise and be content until it was time to eat supper. Supper was always chicken with kibble and very tasty it was too. Of course, we always picked out the chicken first. We were like Thumper and his blossoms in the story Bambi.

One activity that my people continued to do daily was our side-by-side rides. We LOVE those rides! We had the wind whipping through our fur every evening. It was a crazy and wild time for all of us.

I believe it was better than the roller coaster ride at Six Flags. ***Yahoo! We actually thought our ears would fly off. They never did!***

I have a great life here.
I have lived through COVID, the loss of a big brother, and the gain of five siblings. As the oldest, it is my job to be responsible and sensible. I'm good at my job and take it seriously. I'm now four years old, which is twenty-eight in people-years. I don't really pay attention to the twenty-eight because being four is more fun. My siblings don't know the difference.

All they know is that I am their BIG sister. If you are a BIG sister or brother, take your job seriously.

Often I can smell Mallard's scent in the air and I know he is watching over me. I try to do a good job and make him proud.

It is never easy being the oldest, but somebody has to do it. My people give me more freedom and choices than the LITTLE ones get. Always remember that whether you are BIG or LITTLE you are still really important in the lives of others. So, all you BIG sisters and brothers get out the recipe and gather the siblings to bake teacakes.

Have fun and be HAPPY because there is enough SAD in the world.

Here at Corgi Acres
"HAPPINESS"
is one more Corgi!

Meet *Leroy Parker Thompson*
born April 7, 2024, in Chuckey, Tennessee.
He came to live with us at five
and one half months old.

About the Author

Tracy Thompson retired after working thirty years with the State of Georgia. She is celebrating forty years of marriage to her husband Mark. She is the mother of one and Mawmaw to two. She loves to read, write, and garden. She is in her 27th year of teaching Sunday School and is of the Pentecostal faith. She is an active member of *Friends of the Library* and Authors, *Illustrators and Artist.*

She resides in Haralson County, Georgia, with her husband and seven Corgi fur babies. She loves children and this book was written in the hope that it will be enjoyed for years to come.

Tracy's Teacakes

2 c SR flour { add to liquid and stir until thick *
1 c sugar } Beat together first then add other liquids
3 eggs
2 tbsp vanilla
2/3 c soft butter (melted)

I use mini muffin pans to make 36 uniform pieces that are easy to package and don't crumble. Makes 36. Bake at 375° for 15m-18m depending on desired brown-crispness.

* if batter is too sticky to spoon, just add 1 tbsp oil.

"Any Georgia cook, worth her salt, knows she can add flavors or modify to suit her family and the world won't stop spinning"

ENJOY!

About the Illustrator

Stacy Jordon has been an artist her entire life, finding inspiration in everything around her. Unlike specializing in one medium or subject, she fearlessly explores various techniques, creating diverse artwork that reflects her unique style. From realistic portraits to whimsical storybook illustrations, Stacy's art knows no bounds.

Her optimistic outlook on life shines through her art, celebrating the beauty and magic found in the world. Stacy's never-ending creativity leads her on an ongoing adventure of self-discovery, constantly seeking new ways to express herself artistically.

Embracing life to the fullest, Stacy feels incredibly blessed to share her journey. She illustrates children's books with her delightful vision and boundless imagination, captivating young hearts with a visual wonderland.

www.ArtbyStacyJ.com

www.ingramcontent.com/pod-product-compliance
Lightning Source LLC
LaVergne TN
LVHW070437070526
838199LV00015B/535